EVERYONE COMING TOWARD YOU

EVERYONE COMING TOWARD YOU

Poems

David Petruzelli

Tupelo Press
Dorset, Vermont

Everyone Coming Toward You
Copyright © 2005 David Petruzelli
ISBN-10   1-932195-15-7
ISBN-13   978-1-932195-15-6
Printed in Canada
All rights reserved.
No part of this book may be reproduced without the permission of the publisher.

First paperback edition May 2005
Library of Congress Control Number 2004114636
Tupelo Press
PO Box 539, Dorset, Vermont 05251
802.366.8185 • Fax 802.362.1883
editor@tupelopress.org • web www.tupelopress.org

Cover and text designed by Howard Klein

for Margaret Reisner (1960-2000)

Contents

Third Graders Waiting for Thunder

We grew quiet
when we heard it, or maybe
we were quiet already
and then we heard it,

but the unaccustomed dark
helped us bow our heads;
the classroom lights were welcome.
I think we grew quiet then

and began to concentrate,
as though this was September
and we would behave.

But the sound outside continued.
It was something we had to hear again.

I

Father Listens to the Artists

When I was eight months old, Jackson Pollock
stuck his hand in my crib and let me squeeze
one of his fingers. He was in my parents' kitchen
in Hoboken, where we lived for three years;
he said the new linoleum reminded him
of one of his paintings. Every time my mother
tells the story, she always adds, "this is true;"
but my mother can't tell stories.
And my father has stopped remembering.
What never changes is my hand touching Pollock's
and who was watching: my parents and my father's
best friend from childhood—Nick Carone,
a painter who had brought along his famous pal
partly to show off, partly in the hope
Pollock would notice that the work my parents
loyally hung in our living room was Nick's.
But all Pollock cared about, my mother says,
was how much beer was left, how much money
Nick could con my father into giving them,
until the bottles on the table clinked happily
and the artists looked at each other
like lovers who had forgotten our world.
Then Nick placed his hands on my father's shoulders,
Pollock called over to my mother,
who had gone to my crib. Without looking up
she broke her train of baby talk to say goodbye,
but watched my father follow them out
into the hall and stand at the top of the stairs,
waiting as both men began the long walk down.
It's at this point my mother always stops to ask,
Do I remember we lived on the fifth floor?
And by now I've learned to answer, yes I do.

Learning to Play Pool with Vincent

On my best day there were bored 12-year-olds
who could have beaten me, and this was when I practiced
early in the morning before work, and evenings after
dozing in my office or staring at one yellowed wall,
trying to pick out the places where my failed
predecessor had hung his daughter's watercolors,
wondering yet again if letting them face the sun
was the real reason they fired him. Back then
I wrote copy at a science house whose editors let me
crib from authors' questionnaires or examine
the dust jackets of the forgotten or ancient dead,
reading them over until something stirred inside
and for a long time I knew what was expected of me.
Back then I was able to work alone, and few knocked
on my door and no one came to my apartment
in New Jersey, or even knew my living room
had nothing more than a Brunswick pool table
whose slate bed was carried up the stairs in three parts.
The green baize I always babied with a plastic spread,
but when I wasn't there I remembered the cover
slowly roused itself, and in the late morning sun
the brushed green glowed once more, almost new.
On my desk I kept a small framed print of van Gogh's *Night Café,*
where the owner in a white coat stands by his table
like a proud barber expecting the next customer,
while three balls—one red, two white—look earthbound
and lonely, a single cue stick laid out invitingly
as it points to the back room, or wherever the past

keeps itself this evening. Beneath his gaze
I wrote on yellow legal pads in a hand
that came to resemble the finely-meshed crosswriting
of someone's Victorian aunt; by the end of the day
even I couldn't read it. My colleagues included
a doctor's son on loan from our London office
who when he first saw the van Gogh, picked it up
and muttered "rubbish," then politely wondered
if I played. The next evening in a hall downtown
we both noticed my eyesight suddenly weaken,
the air beneath the lights darken, and I knew I was destined
to practice in secret. Back then I came to work
with blue chalk on my fingers and thought of Vincent,
how two years after he had painted the café owner
he lay in a casket set down on a billiard table
in Auvers, while friends brought offerings of sunflowers,
dahlias and pipe tobacco. Two years later
someone would uncover the truth of my resumé,
but for now I practiced day and night, watching the balls
break off into constellations, and pretending I was wild.

Story

I work for someone who remembers Carl Stalling
playing organ in a Kansas City movie house,
how he'd just sit there in the dark and suddenly
out would come these notes like he'd been saving them all week—
music no one would ever miss but everyone agreed
was true to what was up there on the screen.
And in the same story even the red velvet of the seats
remains; Harold Lloyd, he says, was an event.
Meaning the lobby was the frontispiece for a vision;
meaning he remembers something I can't.
At forty I am half his age, with this neatness hinting
at significance—the kind we leave suspended in the air
unexplained: a question mark or exclamation point
as tangible as one that Felix the Cat
made use of just by reaching above his head.
"Gotcha," the music said. "Gotcha," my boss says,
one arm beneath his desk, another pen or pencil
his again, then slipping away, while a look
asks luck to intervene, as though he isn't sure
his hand will come back looking the same. Two years ago
this was no big thing, but now we watch without wanting to,
tense from his efforts at bending down—refusing all help
except the chair's. But when he settles back, he knows
he can relax, and maybe he'll forget there's work,
because the music starts, the dark inside a theater takes over,
and up in the balcony a girlfriend unbuttons his pants.
This is just the sort of detail he knows I like,
and which none of the women get to hear. But then the phone rings,
the girl is gone, and some of us go back to work,

and I'm thinking about my father, how I never heard him tell
a single story about girls or dates or getting laid.
How one Easter everyone's visiting, and my father—
who's just turned off the TV—hoping to deter my niece
from singing "The Easter Parade," starts telling me
one Sunday we're on Fifth Avenue, it's warm,
I'm almost two and in a carriage he has taken charge of
while my mother walks by windows, and coming toward us
is a tall man in Sunday coat and hat, pushing a carriage
and so pleased to be doing it that even my mother turns to look,
and everyone sees who it is—it's John Carradine,
and now he and my father smile, the actor bowing slightly,
slowing just enough to let my father do the same,
each seeing what was required
if two strangers pushing carriages should pass each other,
both agreeably proper, winking at elegance like brand-new cars,
both unimaginably young.
                         And now I see myself,
I think I remember: the Sunday morning light brought back,
the part of a song that gets saved with just three words:

on the avenue

Show & Tell

My fifth grade teacher Mrs. Levy
saw him one Sunday on "First Auditions,"
an amateur hour in the early 1960s
of such continual and unrepentant badness
I remember forgoing morning cartoons
just to watch it. I wasn't sure why my grandfather,
a magician who was once on *Ed Sullivan*,
and still performed at VFWs throughout New Jersey,
would have wanted to appear on the same bill
with singing doormen or a 4-year-old girl
who tap danced to a recording of "Creole Love Call."
But everyone in our family was watching,
and Mrs. Levy still remembered a paper of mine
describing him at our house on my birthday:
the costume he wore, the tricks that kept coming,
the smiling boy emerging from the Chinese box
unharmed. In truth, it hadn't been my birthday,
and the only magic he performed I remembered
as something casual, almost as if he explained
beforehand that what he'd be doing would be just that—
casual, though I know it was only my mother
—when we talked about it later—saying
"sleight of hand," and how the phrase had stayed with me,
touching the back of my neck, as though whenever
I wanted to I could watch him—his hand alighting
from our kitchen drawer along with one deck of cards,
a letter opener, and three ivory dominoes.
Now Mrs. Levy wanted him to come to class.
I thought of our room on the first floor,

with a view of the front lawn, the steps
leading up, and the sounds of whoever was late.
When he came, he came because behind my back
Mrs. Levy called my mother. I was too shy
to throw myself between them. But while he was there
I couldn't enjoy it like the others.
"Relax," said a hypnotist one day,
when he visited our class. I couldn't relax.
"You're on a train," and he described the car
we rode in, how crowded and warm it was,
the cigar smoke blowing in our direction.
"You're feeling a terrible thirst," and the girl
who sat behind me had moaned, like a patient
in the distance, while in the waiting room
we wondered who was next.
I waited to be hypnotized. When my grandfather
performed, I wanted to close my eyes
and pretend we were on a trip out west—
the desert going on and on, a distant silo
high as his hat. And when our train
went into a tunnel, I knew the sun would cool itself
in rivers, or slip easily over each mountain
while another trick arrived: the dark upon us
as simple as a basket closing over me. I lay inside,
on a stage—his volunteer who waited for each sword
to enter. I closed my eyes. I wanted him to begin.

Fog Avenue

In junior high I'd wait forever
for the city bus, or I walked two miles home,
or better yet stopped off to smoke a joint
in Bobby Tyler's bedroom before his mother
returned, or maybe the bus would finally
arrive, and one time I sat in back
along with a baby-faced priest, an abandoned
shopping cart filled with magazines and what
looked like old bones, and across from us two girls
in matching blue skirts of another school.
I tried to listen, but they were whispering,
and one girl looked in my direction
as if her friend explained what I was doing here,
narrating, just for her, this scene:
I noticing her, she noticing me,
both of us seeing the same city.
I told myself I should have spoken,
but that was later. Mostly my encounters
with girls and women occurred this way—
mysterious and uninformed, unlikely
as 14-year-old Ray Bradbury meeting
W.C. Fields, the great man eyeing him,
then handing back the boy's autograph book
with a cheerful, "Here you go, you little son of a bitch,"
the voice not complicated by tenderness,
or how he felt that morning, trying to get up.
For years Fields used to tell the story
how he started out one morning, driving
with a friend from Eastport, Long Island

to Manhattan, in heavy fog that didn't want
to lift, both men drunk of course, but still
managing to keep on. They drove for hours
until they began to wonder how much longer,
driving because they were afraid to stop,
afraid they wouldn't find out how this ended,
and now Fields saw a stranger walking
from his mailbox and asked him how much
further was New York, and the man after
a long moment said "Mister, you're in Georgia."

*

My father once said he thought his voice
sounded different in fog. He felt
it made him sound unsure, leaving a faint taste
in his mouth, like brass he said, or well water.
Whenever we found ourselves in fog
he'd continue to drive, only slower,
his shoulders looking hunched and small,
his silence growing, different from ours,
less afraid, or maybe more afraid than us;
please decide, we said on the way home.

Sunrise Escorts

I used to tell people I quit school
to drive three nights a week
for an escort service on Long Island.
This actually happened, though ten years
went by before I took the job;
it just sounds better the first way
—less lonely. But in the summer
of 1980, using my own car,
a roll of quarters, and the loan
of a beeper, I listened
to Long Island stations tuned impatiently
each night by Darcey—who was eighteen
but spoke in the drifting, nasal tones
of someone dotty and once famous,
while behind me Crystal—who was married
and got the biggest tips—dozed between dates,
or underneath her towel
changed outfits like a child at the beach.
Three nights a week I sat outside
motel rooms or someone's house,
the wife away and one light telling
where their bedroom was. Or someone single
might surprise me with his straight good looks
and a girl on each arm, telling me,
"You take good care of them, okay?"
—my car around the block before I realized
he had wanted to show us he was nice,
to see how all this happened every night
and watch us disappear. Then he could imagine
other men—preceding him, or still ahead,

and they, in turn, trying not to picture him
—his looks and manners, and the neighbors
peeking out to catch it all. His evening was over
as ours started up again,
with distant traffic drawn to growing louder,
and Crystal's lighter lifted up once more,
its one-two click that seemed to put our talk
on hold, until she blew smoke out...
And some nights Darcey teased me,
telling Crystal it was my turn now,
not even touching me to say it, but for once
letting the radio alone while I drove,
as though as dawn got near, her thoughts
grew gentle, and she forgot which songs out there
she didn't like, or didn't want me to hear.

The Visit

There are enough trees to make us forget we have neighbors,
or that later I'll get back to being serious,
like the slow song you never really cared for
finally getting its turn when you're too tired
to do anything but listen. Out by the pool
an old man suns himself quietly among his daughter's friends,
not hearing anyone as he thinks about sleep,
while I'm thinking about the ride home later,
when songs on the radio glide into each other
like a dreamy notion of lovers, and city voices
succeed in reaching us long before we see their lights.
The change from one station's music to another
appears at rare moments seamless, as though the same song
was still with us, only this is the slow part,
and for a few minutes we decide that nothing has changed,
like the uncle who greets me at family gatherings
as if I were still in the fifth grade, and any joke about my height
utterly original. Then I smile the same way for him,
one eye searching for the door, and remember the ride home;
always it's late, and you close your eyes while I want to.

Each time you wake there is never any sleep in your voice.
It's as though you simply pick up where we left off,
and once in the car you opened your eyes and suddenly asked me
whatever happened to the Milky Way, as though we drove past
a row of townhouses and you were reminded of a roller rink
that once stood there, recalling a place instead of stars,
which really aren't gone but just different
from when we were children, the deeply felt sky
others go to the country to see as we go to see friends.

Today they've invited us to sit outside with them,
to say hello to people we've never met or haven't seen in years,
and I imagine that the old man stretched out in his chair
is already dreaming about this Sunday
while everyone around him plays—his day cloudless,
perfect blue of pool and sky; a breeze coming just this way
with a song from somewhere in the house. And eyes
behind shades—dark as pine trees saying "Paradise,"
as all this comes to an end.

II

Afternoon Soaps

The Next Hour

After lunch we looked her way
and watched the motes of dust

like seconds free of the clock
or minutes still milling about,

then listened to the hum of lights
with music practice down the hall.

And when the windows were raised
our wall maps billowed like sails

and still it wasn't time to go.
And when the next breeze came

we saw the papers on her desk
move closer,

and now they were ready
to be handed out.

The Meeting

This was the kind of life that needed help,
an afternoon when the rain was warm and unexpected,

when there was a familiar walk toward feelings,
and he met her at a place

where just the bar was open
and the owner served them, then excused himself

as though he had been paid to disappear,
and for the longest time no one else came in.

She told him she had never answered ads before,
and was still unsure except she'd heard hello

and here she was. He said the best letter
had been hers, the last one he would answer.

There were women who had written out of loneliness,
whose letters would sometimes begin

"I am writing to you out of loneliness,"
from Lufkin, Texas, above a shoe store;

from Island Pond, Vermont, with a copy of her resumé
and a Polaroid of her parents' farm.

But today was like meeting an old friend.
There was happiness here, even if he spoke of it,

in the sudden spring rain, in the shadows
a cat turned his back on while sleeping,

even in the two men who came in
and talked quietly, waiting patiently for the owner

who was off setting tables and let some cutlery
slip from his hand and strike the floor.

But when he heard it she had suddenly looked at her watch
and said it was getting late, but yes

he could call her again, and he thought of the women
whose letters were adventurous and moving

but on the phone they spoke as though he'd caught them
as they were about to go to sleep

or as they were going out, and when he called again
he thought the red eye of each answering machine

recognized persistence, and when he stayed behind
it was just to finish his drink and watch her leave,

the check stirring gently from their table,
the wet street filled with sunlight and ways to meet women.

Afternoon Soap

I'm too young to stay outdoors alone.
The stray glove left on the sidewalk

—I mustn't touch it.
I can't poke the dead pigeon.

Tears come easily. In our apartment
my mother hurries to the kitchen,

the radio comes on; an organ plays.
Already she's enjoying the story:

the man's voice gets close to her;
the woman sounds afraid of music;

their day grows overcast. Two rooms away,
under my pillow, I still hear them—

it's like the sound of water
as I drink from a fountain in the park.

Head bowed, eyes closed, for a moment you hear
everyone who was there before you.

Her Every No

Maybe it's easier to buy new clothes
rather than wash the old,

to let her boyfriend entertain himself
while she dozes on the couch all afternoon,

and now he wanders through each room,
pausing to view the cartons of old take-outs

and retrieve her underwear—all yellows
and pale blues—folding them, starting to remember.

Afterwards he sits down with that book
on ballet—once a favorite of hers

and now, it seems, of his, if only
for the black & white photos of young girls

or the endpapers marbled by hand in Paris,
and which he touches now

as if nothing found on her floor could compare.
But at five he says, "I'll call you later,"

and even though he's standing over her
she'll remember his voice

as coming from the hall; her eyes closing
forgo the door's rough kiss. She touches her face,

remembers the feel of his hand,
and that earlier she said please come over;

that she had really said please;
that he brushed one cheek as if checking for dust.

The Ocean

She took one look at me
and said Okay, I could be company,

then let me play with her,
the daughter of my mother's friend,

the both of us in bathing suits
and one puddle of a pool

I stepped in and out of,
wondering where the fun might be.

I was four and hated being here.
I remember a yard without trees,

that we couldn't go inside the house,
that she was older.

On the patio, our mothers
sat beneath a white umbrella,

a pitcher of iced tea waiting for us,
as though part of a plan

to get me to come closer.
Instead, I noticed in the grass

a garden hose, and made believe
I didn't see it

while all three read my mind;
but I got there first

and calmly turned the nozzle on
as though they shouted instructions

instead of my name. Then I hit
the house, the open windows, the girl.

I made her run to the cellar
to shut the water off,

find the one loose step to slip on,
then fall into storm windows

kept by the foot of the stairs.
Now our mothers hurried past;

they ran right through me,
their one voice saying: Don't move.

But I watched from the top of the stairs.
I waited for her crying to stop,

then dried myself off and dressed,
I lifted up one floorboard

in a house built over the ocean
and looked down. Then I came home and slept.

Lunch Hour

When the others have gone, he can look up
at the clock, the way he might have sat

in a hotel lobby, and watched the gold
old-fashioned arrow of each elevator

gently rise and fall, someone who recalls
red carpets, and elevator boys perched on stools

as if being punished. And when he sees her
—a young woman he has noticed for several days—

she steps in, alone:
the doors stay open, and knowing he wants her

they close, while he waits like a detective
her husband or boyfriend hired, feeling closer

as the arrow climbs calmly and stops. And seeing
which floor she goes to is suddenly enough,

even when the hour's over and everyone is back,
and he returns to something open on his desk.

Memories of My Paper Route

He says he sees me riding
my bicycle, five blocks away,

but I always have to wait
while he looks for change.

Lowering the TV, he asks
if I want something to drink,

and he's still there on his porch
as I ride down the street.

By now he knows how much I earn,
that each paper wears a plastic sleeve

even if there isn't rain—just like
my father, and his father before him;

that one night an old woman
answered her door naked

and all I could do was say,
"You owe for three weeks."

I see he's lonely but I remind him—
it's almost dark, and I have to be home.

The Advice of Noon

He says at 80, one shouldn't have to wait
to be seated, or open a menu

only to hear the talk at other tables—
where each word bears the fine dust of an anecdote,

and someone admiring his white beard says
he looks like a Confederate general on Sunday.

This he'll cherish, knowing when the maitre d'
without a word pulled out his chair for him,

others saw it as more impressive than a sword
being drawn. Then the room resumed its talking,

as though from the opening of his napkin
came permission, and no one he saw

took notice that he always dines alone.
But someone has to drive him, run errands,

watch over him and sometimes it's me;
next stop: Atlantic City. I'll hear on the way

about Vegas starting to simmer in the fifties,
or Texas barbecues on weekend passes,

and women with nicknames like outlaw musicians.
On winning days he wishes he were younger,

but every time we go he's at the tables all night,
and at the hour when he rings my room

it's to have me help him from bed,
even though when I arrive

he sits there with the smile of the false alarm,
as if someone else had gotten there first,

someone who whispered in his ear, reminding him:
patience feels like sunlight.

Thunder Reminiscence

The clouds assembled, the lights came on
as if here were evening,

when parents would call us home.
They enjoyed the ease in saying, "Let's go,"

the ambiguity of, "It's time,"
knowing how each of these underscored

the sudden loss of light,
the children preaching disappointment,

the park abandoned. But those who stayed behind
were about to know something we wouldn't.

In the dark they were unafraid,
and while we ate supper

they grew up, moved away—
no longer our friends, arriving in a city

we never saw, but sometimes listened to.
And now, late afternoons on a terrace,

the sky is sepia, the sounds
of traffic far below, almost soothing.

And someone is thinking fondly
of the woman he met for lunch;

her smile, her use of the word *wicked*
to describe her life.

Explanations

Voices that cannot be our own
when we put them in the world

go on. In the afternoon rain
they've gone at it for two blocks,

she shouting, the man simply trying
to walk, not quite beside her

as if he hopes a show of deference
might soften her,

except she's past feeling
the slightest changes in her favor:

the rain lighter, or the man's silence
gaining on him. And when

the sound of traffic seems to lift,
it lets her hear herself

as he'll remember it, allowing her
to choose right now to say,

"How do you think *I* feel?"
then says again, "How do you think *I* feel?"

—knowing once she's allowed to repeat
her words, to say and hear them

in her own sweet time, means
she'll always be the one who tells the story…

I'll hear her later, when I get home,
in the time spent opening the door,

long enough to make up a woman's voice:
"Get out of those wet clothes, dear."

For now, it's all I require of her.
As I start to undress

I shiver slightly, knowing
I'm about to lie down, knowing

no one will wake me.
I tell myself—I always do—

it will only be for a short while.
But then I open my eyes, slowly

or suddenly, it doesn't matter;
the afternoon is over.

And I feel strange the room is dark.
I want to be the one who tells the story.

III

The Conch in the Next Life

The time you spoke to no one,
made a fist and years later
woke up—remember?

Like a swimmer lying down
exhausted, in the sun,
you still feel it, the waves still working.

Miles of seaweed shrug with the surf.
Fossil starfish burn on the rocks
like blaze marks. And again

your breath slips back to tell you:
do not give yourself up.

Interpretations of the Door

I was trying to remember *Dressed to Kill*,
and whoever played the husband—the one
Angie Dickinson and even the director
seemed bored with: that's who used to own the cabin
my friend Thomas moved into one summer.
When he told me, this was years ago,
this was late at night, with cartons still standing
in unfinished pyramids, a 12-pack nearly done.
Wicker love seats the actor left behind
appeared as giant fishing creels; in one corner
a spider as big as a walnut.
For a long time it sat perfectly still,
then like someone who's done nothing at their desk
yet senses being watched—it went to work again.
"Blink twice," he said, "you'd miss him," as I switched on
a lamp, but he meant the actor's meager part.

In my parents' house, a light on late at night
upset my father; music turned low upstairs
seemed to trouble him. He always thought
someone was in my room, talking gently
and smoothly. Someone undressing me.
When my father knocked, I was always alone.
He looked confused, he looked like someone
who, if they were a little more awake,
would tell me to look for a job.
When I explained I was going to sleep,
when I told my father *soon*, he always understood,
and went away. He knew where I was,

he was happy. He knew his sleep was somewhere nearby.

Fred Webber, Angie's lover for just one day
of filming, brought a different girl each weekend;
the neighbors saw things, they told us stories.
I could see my father waking, sitting
at the edge of the bed, his eyes still closed.
Very soon, he'd come halfway up the stairs
and listen for me. In the woods, I pictured
my parents' house, the early light, no one outside,
my father still sleeping. It would never get any later.

Stephanie Above

Twice now she passed out while her bathtub ran water
through his ceiling. And one time she came home at 5 AM
thinking his door was hers as she tried out different keys
then kicked hard, just once, before she went upstairs
very slowly, as if she thought there was a chance
the door would change its mind. And one evening
he found her asleep in the building's foyer,
but saying her name he saw a beginner's smile on her face
and very gently shook her, finally getting her
to go up the stairs, his hands on her shoulders, his best voice
suggesting each step, praying they would reach her floor
before anyone saw them, someone wondering what he had done
to her or made her do. Upstairs he kept her from falling
while he searched through her bag, reaching down
where strangers huddled in steerage and soft things
left his fingers, and just before he found her keys
he pulled out a photo post card from the gallery she ran
showing Quentin Crisp lying on a leather couch,
a nearly naked woman with long blond hair beside him,
a whip at their feet. He palmed the card.
                                    And only later—
after he told her she was home, and helped with her boots,
hung up her coat and went back downstairs
—did he look at the card again, and the woman
with Quentin, and the book he held open for them,
her face like someone trying to learn,
the old man tired and amused. On the back he read about
the long photo shoot—his very last, and the woman,
Nicki Chase, "a performance artist and dominatrix,"

and the photographer lauding their patience,
and only when he turned to the picture again
did he realize the woman on the couch
was Stephanie. He stared up at the ceiling.

One night when she had come home, he heard her door shut,
and footsteps cross the room, then right above his head
a single heavy boot struck the floor. Late at night
it was the only sound, it was like a warning,
and he found himself waiting, but he never heard
the other one, he never heard Stephanie again that night.
And before he fell asleep he tried to picture her
passed out in her chair, or on the bed, or only
remembering the hour and now taking the other boot off
slowly, teasingly, as if reminding herself
that once she set the boot down, if she placed it
on the floor very carefully, then she never had to leave.

The Lesson

Late August, Cape Cod. It's 30 years ago,
and a girl my age (I've just turned ten)
listens one night to her well-dressed father

as he tries to teach her the fine points
of miniature golf. He's patient,
she's pretty, which is why I've noticed her.

The instructions he whispers
seem small endearments which make her smile.
She never says a word, but on the seventh green

she sinks her ball in one smooth shot
and makes a sound, covering her mouth
like one who promised not to laugh then does.

On the fairway, three ornamental gnomes
applaud. But there's her father—he's serious,
and brings one finger to his lips.

Somehow I know I will always add the words
"she spoke"—and I will always be wrong.
We might be playing together

on a day after school, when we each
discover what it sounds like
when you take hold of your tongue

and try to speak. That's all I hear.
Her father looks so sad, as other children giggle,
or aren't sure they should, and grown-ups

stand in silence, then start to talk again,
knowing they have changed the subject.
I let her and her father play on ahead.

It's like the summer's calmest night,
when a neighbor's cat—the one we thought
we knew—suddenly in heat, lets go,

and its awful cry for one bold instant
stops us from breathing.
It's like the summer's calmest night,

the girl and her father still playing.

Hello and Goodbye

When we go around the room
reciting names in Monday morning
group, she's waiting. It's when
the young man sitting next to her
says his name that I start to notice,
how she's playing with her hair
as though she wants to raise
a sound from it. "I'm Karen,"
she finally tells us, then adds
to get it over with,
"I tried to kill myself last night,"
and remembers, in the distance,
last night, even as some of us
doze in our chairs, or look toward
the door, wanting lunch or a way home.
But last night a woman came in
like a half-wakened child pulled from bed,
to a place where grown-ups stood
outside her room, their concern
whispered, like doctors sharing
only with themselves. They waited,
but when the oldest caught us looking
he smiled, and then I knew
this was her father, and the news
when it came, could come as near
as it wished, and so could I.
Now it's morning, time to take
my morning-colored pills, to find
my favorite chair and tell no one;
time to go back to my room
and dream of another home.

There the shower never hesitates,
new sheets smell of lovemaking,
and a woman half my age
smiles at a vase of yellow roses
while she smokes in my presence
the first of many cigarettes.

Time to wake up.
But one night we sit outside
for as long as we're allowed,
not friends at first, not friends
exactly, but friends—at home
in a found world where hospitals
look like ski lodges, where the woods
come close to help us sleep,
and in the parking lot each weekend
visitors step from their cars,
already sighing, about to begin.
The question they will always ask you
is, When are you going home?
And they have their answer
when you are far enough from here
to wave goodbye. And later,
when I've gone to sleep, when she's sure
everyone is sleeping, she'll wave too.

What I Do to Them

By the time I entered high school
I had two teachers who killed themselves:
both were women, both started up their cars
with the garage door shut, both times
we didn't get a single day off.
When they told us about Mrs. Needham
my seventh grade homeroom teacher,
the principal asked us to close our books
and fold our hands. He sounded sad but helpful,
he wanted us to sit in silence,
though underneath, a more familiar voice
was saying: *God help the boy or girl*
who can't be serious for five minutes.
I thought once he saw us—the rows and rows
of respectful faces, saw how truly solemn
we could be, the rest of the day
would surely come over to our side
and we could go home. I sat up straight,
I listened as Peggy Wheeler, who sat
behind me and cried easily, made a sound
like half praying and half inhaling of food.
I heard the other homerooms pick up
their voices and go farther down the hall.
I began to pay attention to the flagpole,
the rigging that clanged in the wind,
and after two minutes I was tired
of my quiet and everyone else's.
I never liked Mrs. Needham. I kept wishing
someone would raise their hand and ask,
"Does this mean we can have a party?"

I hated the hour we had to sit
through Homeroom, wondering when I would
hear my name, and how I would hear it,
only to return every afternoon
and sit in the same seat—the room smaller now—
unprepared for History, bored with English,
waiting as her voice—flat, impatient,
out-of-print—cut short a seventh grader's sigh.

My other teacher, Mrs. Longobardi,
I can barely remember, other than being
in second grade, and that one weekend
I saw her at the local park.
My mother says I worshiped her, meaning
the woman I saw seriously each day
wasn't old, wasn't married, or at 32
already had three boys, each born—one year
apart—with cerebral palsy.
But add she was deeply Catholic, believed
after each birth she hadn't prayed enough,
and one morning found her husband's
parting words in a No. 10 envelope
to be eaten with breakfast, and you know
what I was never told in the second grade.
All I pictured were three boys wakened
in the middle of the night, helped
into their clothes as she tells them—
time for your Sunday drive, then carries them
to the back seat of her car. In a dream
all I see is Mrs. Longobardi
on a worn green bench, squinting at sunshine
like a teacher searching for her desk,
the just-mowed grass of Albion Place Park

around us. In one hand she holds
an open book, youngest on her lap,
the other boys sit on either side
as she calls to me. Now I know
she has a life outside. Now I'm happy.
It's hearing her say my name,
it's the way sunlight falls. It's her not caring
what I do to each of them by waking.

Premonitions

In memory, Oliver Hardy stands,
not quite at home
in a kitchen he is doomed to wreck.

Shy and shamefaced, like a boy caught in a lie
which now seems labyrinthine, he is menaced
by his wife, who is half his size;

she has forgotten this is only a story.
At the age of five, I was frightened
by her anger—the inescapable pots and pans,

her rolling pin like a week of papers
delivered all at once. His punishment:
their marriage without end.

This he would remember like his hat.
I thought of him whenever girls my age
acted serious, whenever they put on

their mothers' perfume. I think of Stan Laurel,
the one who chose wisely, whose smile meant
he'd always be forgiven—

now holding his nurse's hand,
sounding like a child about to tell
his latest secret, though all he did was sigh,

"I wish I were skiing." She felt relieved.
"You never told me you could ski." "I can't," Laurel said,
"but I'd rather do that than this." Then he died.

For Once in Her Short Life, Singing

Each time I keep it simple, sort of innocent
if by innocent you mean it never happened—
the club's owner a friend of her father's,
the patrons part-family and part-regulars,
though mostly the latter. At 9:30, waiters
catch meaning in the ruins of ashtrays
and glasses seem to challenge girls
with their clinking, and everyone talks
as if they knew exactly where they were.
Back in her dressing room, I sit with her
while she impatiently goes over lyrics,
studying this or that page as if trying
to pin down what the taste from her cigarette
reminds her of, and getting no further
than deciding I shouldn't be here,
yet softening her left cheek as I kiss her
and leave. Few have heard her before,
and no one will know if she cuts her set short
or whether she's good enough to be
invited back, though she will never be
invited back. But every table is taken,
and from the rear I always imagine
the moment the lights go, and the way
they take voices with them, even the ones
who say they'll return. And now it's just her,
which means a single light on her face,
and a voice that isn't sure how much she wants this;
doesn't know how long I want it to go on.

The Park Keeper

There is nothing to wish for—just happiness,
and other children in a morning underway, the trees
placed as sparingly as lampposts, the park bench

chosen for a grandmother's view. And Grandma
with our lunch and a time to be back, and her trick
of opening *McCall's*, reading for a minute or two

then hearing the voice of a friend, always someone
she hadn't seen in twenty years. Each time
I visited, she took us to a different park:

I ran to play, I ran where everyone was.
There was no one who I knew, no one I remember now
except an old man mistaking me for someone else,

maybe watching as I passed him, looking as I climbed,
joined the mob of children on the jungle gym.
But they were quiet when he called, waved me over

with his stick still jammed with papers from the grass:
"I thought I told you not to come here anymore."
A voice so serious, I don't remember if I breathed,

only the playground's blacktop talking back,
and pigeons breaking up their game of kickball
—just to watch me go. I remember my mother

telling me how one day she skipped school
to go to the movies, then stayed on to watch
one film again—a romance she wanted for herself,

but at her favorite part, where the man and woman
are standing at her door, and for the first time
he's about to kiss her goodnight, my mother overheard

the boy sitting behind her whisper to his friends,
He can't wait to fuck her. And after that
she couldn't stay, she didn't want to watch it anymore.

But sometimes, asleep, I climb up here:
the jungle gym like a building still unfinished,
a place where sleepwalkers, guided by luck,

take steps they hone to a narrow few.
And when I want to leave, I meet a man,
and see in his lifting of leaves a burlap bag,

and inside, folded, a lawn which comes alive
like a blanket shook clean,
the wet grass in a darkness it forgets.

When I couldn't sleep, I only wished I knew
if I should go to him, say to his face
that he was crazy, then run. And safely turning

I'd watch for him. I would always be far away.

The Night Nurse Says Goodnight

Beds peeked out from curtains
the color of weak tea, and behind them
my mother would visit her aunt.

I said hello inside that ward
where grown-ups hid from children.
But here is cheerlessness upgraded,

by adding stripes. The curtains stir
wherever there's talk, and in bed
a woman sits up with visitors,

holding a cup filled with ice
she eats a piece at a time,
thinking, *one swallow and this friend leaves,*

another one and that friend goes.
Above her they chat among themselves
but finally she closes her eyes,

as if listening to water
at the bottom of her cup—which I take
from her. Now everyone has left.

Hallway

The "new" wing in grade school wasn't new
even when I went there,
and that was forty years ago, yet whenever
I dream about school, afterwards
that's still the way I think of it.
It's reassuring I remember:
the mustard yellow of the halls,
the girl's face as she turned from the others
still studying. The way the desks lined up,
expecting us. It's useless knowledge,
like recalling a bookseller's sky blue
lettersheet, when he wrote July 6, 1849:
"Sir I saved the History of the World for you
and you can have it anytime you please.
I should like for you to have it
as I have kept it for you."
Then signed his name. I read that
just once, at a house sale in New Hampshire
as I searched through family papers:
letters, journals, words away at school,
careful bundles I began to see were decades,
each letter unfolding like a napkin.
And I remember, still inside its envelope,
a child's watercolor of a young lady
on horseback. The red of her dress,
the yellow of the house behind her
were still as intended; even sunlight
was somehow saved. *Ephemera: One Carton,*
the lot description read. Late in the day
I lost out. At 28 I was broke

and still lived at home.
But I liked the way horse and rider
turned to stare, the girl's patience while I looked.
I liked how the bookseller was helpful,
even if he wrote this way to everyone.
But if given the choice between
saying "corridor" or "hallway"
—I think he would have sided with me,
because of how dark and narrow the first word
sounds, how the number of syllables
favors a decade much earlier than mine,
one my parents might have walked down
every day, especially my father,
who can only remember very distant things.

When I talk about remembering,
this is what I mean: a hallway in school,
where one girl smiles hello
before friends carry her off
triumphantly, with the sound of bells,
and everyone coming toward you.

Notes

"Story" —The composer Carl Stalling, best known as Musical Director for more than six hundred Warner Brothers cartoons, got his start as an accompanist to silent films. In Kansas City he played organ and conducted a pit orchestra.

"Fog Avenue" —Ray Bradbury met Fields during the filming of *You're Telling Me*. The anecdote is recounted in Ronald Field's *W.C. Fields: A Life on Film*.

The photograph in "Stephanie Above" reimagines one by Gary Azon.

The letter quoted in "Hallway" was written by a 19th century American bookseller, Jacob Hallock.

Acknowledgments

Some of these poems appeared previously in *Barrow Street, The Gettysburg Review, The New Yorker, Partisan Review, Rattle* and *Sulphur River Literary Review.*